PICTURE CREDITS AND CONTRIBUTO

Picture c

The Automobile Association wishes to thank t
for their assistance in the preparation of this b

J.ALLAN CASH PHOTOLIBRARY spine Fountain of Neptune. THE BRIDGEMAN ART LIBRARY, LONDON 28a black figure vase, Bucchero ware, Etruscan, 6th century BC, Museo Archeologico, Chiusi/K & B News Foto, Florence; 39 *Adoration of the Magi* by Sandro Botticelli (1444/5–1510) Galleria degli Uffizi, Florence; 40b *Portrait of Savonarola* by Fra Bartolommeo (c 1472–c 1517) Museo di San Marco dell'Angelico, Florence; 88 *Adoration of the Christ Child with the Young St. John the Baptist* by Pseudo Pier Francesco Fiorentino (fl.1475–1500) Museo Bardini, Florence; 101 *The Annunciation* by Fra Angelico, (c 1387–1455) Museo di San Marco dell'Angelico, Florence; 116 *The Parting of Venus from Adonis*, 1707–1708 (fresco) by Sebastiano Ricci (1658–1734) Palazzo Pitti, Florence; 118 *Portrait of an Unknown Man* (detail) by Titian (Tiziano Vecellio) (c 1485–1576) Palazzo Pitti, Florence; 124b *Portrait of Machiavelli* by Santi di Tito (1536–1603) Palazzo Vecchio, Florence; 145 *Adam and Eve Banished from Paradise* by Tommaso Masaccio (1401–1428) Brancacci Chapel, Santa Maria del Carmine, Florence; 146–147 *St. Peter Visited in Jail by St. Paul*, c 1480 by Filippino Lippi (c 1457/8–1504) Brancacci Chapel, Santa Maria del Carmine, Florence; 161 *The Madonna di Ognissanti*, c 1310 (post-restoration) by Ambrogio Bondone Giotto (c 1266–1337) Galleria degli Uffizi, Florence; 246a Etruscan vase showing boxers fighting c 500BC, British Museum, London. MARY EVANS PICTURE LIBRARY 45b Napoleon I; 74 Pope Sixtus IV; 222a Shelley; 222b Robert Browning. KIT HOARE 45a Tuscan landscape. HULTON DEUTSCH COLLECTION LTD 47 floods, books needing rebinding; 130a floods 1966–1967; 130b floods; 131 flood damage. TIM JEPSON 57 courtyard, Bargello; 108 Museo Zoologico. THE MANSELL COLLECTION LTD 36a Frederick Barbarossa's Court; 36b Frederick Barbarossa; 41 Savonarola; 42b Pope Giovanni de'Medici; 68 Giuliano de'Medici; 75a Giuliano; 75b Lorenzo; 104 instrument, Galileo; 106a Galileo; 106b Galileo; 223a Tobias Smollett; 223b Huxley. ROYAL GEO-GRAPHICAL SOCIETY 43 map. SPECTRUM COLOUR LIBRARY 67 *Madonna and Child* by Michelangelo. DAVID WALSH 102–103 Fra Angelica; 149 *Trinità* by Masaccio. ZEFA PICTURE LIBRARY (UK) LTD 17 Siena, Palio race; 28b figure (Etruscan); 52 interior of Accademia Gallery; 53 *David* by Michelangelo; 240b Siena, Palio race; 241 drummers.

The remaining photographs are held in the Automobile Association's own photo library (AA PHOTO LIBRARY) and were taken by Clive Sawyer, with the exception of the following pages: 16b, 20–21, 20, 24–25, 27, 37, 38a, 48–49, 70a, 77, 80b, 92, 111, 154, 166–167, 182b, 187, 194, 238a, 241, 252, 256a, 258–259, 260a, 263, 271a (Jerry Edmanson); 210b, 211 (Eric Meacher); the cover and pages 4a, 4b, 9, 12b, 19, 26, 30–31, 31b, 56, 66, 80a, 81, 82, 84–85, 148, 151, 152b, 156, 168, 183, 189, 190a, 191, 196–197, 196b, 198, 203, 210a, 212a, 212b, 225, 227a, 228, 229, 230, 231, 232a, 232b, 233, 234, 242, 245, 246b, 248, 251, 262, 267 (Ken Paterson); 73 (James Robertson-Taylor); 7, 49, 151, 162, 175a, 253, 255, 273 (Barrie Smith); 18–19, 181 (Wyn Voysey).

Contributors

Original copy editor: Julia Brittain **Original designer**: Jo Tapper
Revision copy editor/Americanizer: Donna Dailey **Revision verifier**: Tim Jepson
Indexer: Marie Lorimer

44771577643

Fodor's

EXPLORING

FLORENCE
& TUSCANY

FODOR'S TRAVEL PUBLICATIONS, INC.
NEW YORK • TORONTO • LONDON • SYDNEY • AUCKLAND

WWW.FODORS.COM/

Published in the United States by Fodor's Travel Publications, Inc.
Published in the United Kingdom by AA Publishing.

Fodor's and Fodor's Exploring Guides are registered trademarks of Fodor's Travel Publications, Inc.

ISBN 0-679-03205-3
Second Edition

Fodor's Exploring Florence & Tuscany

Author: **Tim Jepson**
Cover Design: **Louise Fili, Fabrizio La Rocca**
Front Cover Silhouette: **BKA/Network Aspen**

Special Sales

Fodor's Travel Publications are available at special discounts for bulk purchases (100 copies or more) for sales promotions or premiums. Special editions, including personalized covers, excerpts of existing guides, and corporate imprints, can be created in large quantities for special needs. For more information, contact your local bookseller or write to Special Markets, Fodor's Travel Publications, 201 East 50th Street, New York, NY 10022. Inquiries from Canada should be directed to your local Canadian bookseller or sent to Random House of Canada, Ltd., Marketing Department, 2775 Matheson Blvd. East, Mississauga, Ontario L4W 4P7.

Printed and bound in Italy by Printer Trento srl
10 9 8 7 6 5 4 3

How to use this book

This book is divided into five main sections:

❏ Section 1: *Florence Is*
Discusses aspects of life and living today, from tourism and restoration to café life

❏ Section 2: *Florence Was*
Places the city in its historical context and explores those past events whose influences are felt to this day

❏ Section 3: *A to Z Section*
Breaks down into two chapters, covering Florence and Tuscany, and covers places to visit, including walks and drives. Within this section fall the Focus On articles, which consider a variety of topics in greater detail

❏ Section 4: *Travel Facts*
Has the strictly practical information vital for a successful trip

❏ Section 5:
Hotels and Restaurants
Lists recommended establishments in Florence and Tuscany, giving a brief summary of what they offer

How to use the star rating
Most places described in this book have been given a separate rating:

▶▶▶ **Do not miss**

▶▶ **Highly recommended**

▶ **Worth seeing**

Not essential viewing

Map references
To make the location of a particular place easier to find, every main entry in this book is given its own map reference, such as 176B3. The first number (176) indicates the page on which the map can be found, the letter (B) and the second number (3) pinpoint the square in which the main entry is located. The maps on the inside front cover and inside back cover are referred to as IFC and IBC respectively.

Contents

6

This quick-reference guide high-lights the features of the book you will use most often: the maps; the introductory features; the Focus On articles; the walks and the drives.

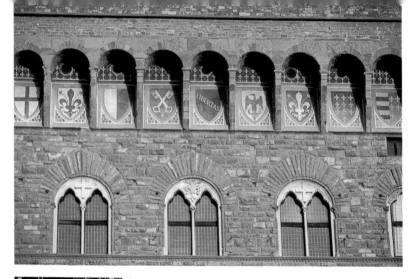

My Florence & Tuscany

by Tim Jepson

Tim Jepson has written or contributed to many books on Italy, including *Wild Italy* (Aurum Press), *Italy by Train* (Hodder & Stoughton), the *Fodor Guide to Italy* and *The Rough Guide to Tuscany & Umbria*, as well as *Rome, Italy* and *Venice* in the AA *Explorer* series. He has also written AA *Explorer Canada* and *Essential Tuscany & Florence*. Tim's future plans include walking the length of Italy and the breadth of the Pyrenees, in addition to exploring South America and the Arctic.

Tuscany for me, I'm afraid, is the Tuscany of popular cliché. Nowhere else can I think of a place where land-scape, art, food, wine and culture come together to create a region so close to perfection. And if Florence, the region's capital, isn't quite the perfect city, then I can't imagine where quite so many of the world's great works of art are gathered together in one place.

I first came to Tuscany 20 years ago, and have been returning every year since. Never in that time have I tired of the paintings, the churches or the cypress-dotted hills. Never have I thought "enough of frescoes"; never felt the silver grey of olive trees, or the verdant green of vines, was anything other than sublimely beautiful. These are land-scapes in which I could live forever. And though this isn't true of Florence (Siena is a different matter), I could happi-ly return to many paintings time and again and find myself endlessly captivated (Fra Angelico's *Annunciation* in San Marco is the one I'd take away with me if I could).

But Florence and Tuscany are not simply about art and landscape. Several years ago I lived near Montalcino, a tiny Tuscan hilltown. Over several drowsy summer months my beautiful pastoral surroundings gradually became nothing more than a backdrop to an idyllic way of life. I visited Pienza, Montepulciano and other of the region's gem-like hilltowns. I explored Romanesque churches and crumbling medieval monasteries. But as time went by, the obvious attractions of art and countryside drifted into the back-ground. Instead I found that my idea of Tuscany began to revolve around more subtle and sedentary pleasures: food – simple and enjoyable; wine – an essential part of the daily routine; coffee – the world's best *cappuccinos*; cafés – just watching the world go by; nightlife – a quiet Campari and the flickering of a thousand fire-flies. The list went on ...

Landscape, art and all the things that make for civilized good living: these are my idea of Florence and Tuscany. The perfect region, the near-perfect city: add in love and a little work, and you'd have the recipe for a perfect life.

FLORENCE IS

■ **Florence is a city-sized shrine to the Renaissance. Its churches, museums, and galleries catalogue an epoch that shaped history and produced some of the greatest works of art of all time. But if you come here only for art and architecture you will have missed the heart of a living city ...■**

Museum city You go to Rome to look at Rome, to Venice to look at Venice, but to Florence to look at paintings—or so it might sometimes seem. As a city to see for its own sake, Tuscany's capital has always ranked below its big Italian rivals. It has no ruins (unlike Rome) and no fairy-tale settings (unlike Venice). Florence, one is told, lacks romance, lacks an atmosphere to call its own. This city has no lost lagoons, no crumbling layers of history. It is neither timeless like Venice, nor eternal like Rome. This is the received wisdom, and being wisdom

A detail of Pietro Tacca's fountain in Piazza Santissima Annunziata

it contains a truth of sorts. If approached in the wrong way Florence *can* seem an indoor city: its sights, for the most part, are concealed within churches and museums. Its streets can, at times, seem gloomy. Its architecture *is* often stolid and forbidding. Seen from a different angle, however, the picture looks very different.

Another side Florence's appeal goes way beyond the world of sculptures and gallery Madonnas. It has a river to give it heart, markets to give it life. Its citizens are proud and stylish (unlike those of Rome), its streets part of a living city (unlike those of Venice). Old-world artisans flourish, and designers—Gucci and Ferragamo the most famous—dress it in a fashion to match Milan. Its cuisine—rustic but refined—is superb, its cafés stylish and sedate. Cultural life abounds: the Maggio Musicale is one of Italy's finest arts festivals. The Giardino di Boboli is Italy's most visited garden (giving the lie to the idea of Florence as an indoor city). And this is without the art, without one of Europe's greatest galleries (the Uffizi), without Michelangelo's *David* or the world's finest Renaissance sculptures (in the Bargello).

Romance Florence is also a city with its share of romance—the Ponte Vecchio, for example, glimpsed across the Arno on a summer's evening; a late-night drink sipped in Piazza della Signoria; the flower-hung streets of the Oltrarno explored on a warm afternoon; or the majestic cityscapes to be enjoyed from San Miniato or Giotto's lofty Campanile. It is also a city to fire the historical imagination.

Picture, for example, Dante, Machiavelli, Boccaccio, and Galileo wandering its streets. Or Lorenzo the Magnificent in the Duomo fleeing his would-be assassins; or Michelangelo striding the city's defenses in preparation for the siege of the city by the combined armies of the emperor and the pope; or Savonarola's huge Bonfire of Vanities crackling in Piazza della Signoria.

Seeing it all At first glance, it might seem that you can see all of Florence within a few days. It is small, and all the sights are close together. Don't be fooled. Every gallery, however modest, is essential; every church a treasure-house of art. A week's stay here is only going to scratch the surface. And that is without the Uffizi, the Bargello, or the churches of Santa Croce and Santa Maria Novella—each worth a whole morning on its own.

Still, you should avoid trying to see more than is pleasurable. Nothing is worse than the misery of museum fatigue. Accept your limitations and pick out the highlights. Plan ahead, don't tackle too much, and avoid the streets in the heat of the afternoon. Head-on confrontation with the city, however energetically you join battle, will always leave you the dispirited loser. Allow time for lounging in gardens, an hour in a sun-drenched café, a quiet meal under a starry sky, or an ice cream from Italy's best *gelateria* (Vivoli). And then, of course, when you have exhausted the city, you have the rest of Tuscany—Italy's most beautiful region—waiting to be explored.

Make time to relax in Florence's beautiful Boboli gardens

■ **Florentines, like any group of Italians, are a breed apart, riddled with their own particular faults and foibles, vices and virtues. Stereotypes are invidious things, but no one meeting a Roman or a Neapolitan, for example, could confuse them with a Florentine ...■**

Foreigners in their own country

Italians are never simply Italians. Centuries of divisive history have left them fiercely provincial, bound by that force known neatly as *campanilismo*—the idea that all that matters is what takes place within the sound of your own church bells, and that everything else belongs to a foreign country. Tuscans are never Italians, therefore—except perhaps when the national soccer team is playing. Nor, however, are they simply Tuscans.

Art, architecture—and daily life

Someone from Siena is Sienese, and proud of the fact; someone from Pisa is Pisan, and woe betide anyone who calls them otherwise.

> ❏ "Beyond all others, a treacherous and mercenary race."
> Walter Savage Landor (1775–1864) ❏

Florentines on Florentines

Michelangelo, who grew up in Florence, said "I never had to do with a more ungrateful and arrogant people than the Florentines." Dante, a native of the city, described his fellow citizens as "*gente avara, invidiosa e superba*" (mean, envious, and proud people). A Renaissance proverb described them as perpetual moaners—possessed of "sharp eyes and bad tongues." Leaving aside personal agendas—Michelangelo was habitually bad-tempered and Dante was exiled by his fellow Florentines—the assessments, if deliberately overpitched for rhetorical purposes, mention qualities still seen today as distinctively Florentine: pride and haughtiness.

> ❏ "Prodigal of cry and gesture when the world goes right."
> Elizabeth Barrett Browning (1806–61) ❏

Florentine pride The proverbial Florentine pride is an affront to many Italians, who wonder what it is, exactly, that makes Florentines regard themselves so highly. The Renaissance, it seems, is one answer, a golden age that merely

12

13

Enjoying the bright lights of Via dei Calzaiuoli

reflects qualities—hard work, genius, flair, ambition, verve, civic pride—that are still possessed by the average Florentine. Certainly there are other reasons—poets, painters and sculptors, scientists and political theorists; Dante and Boccaccio; Botticelli and Michelangelo; Galileo and Machiavelli; Europe's first public library; the western world's first chair of Greek; the creation of a literary language; the rediscovery of perspective; the foundation of capitalism; the invention of opera, eyeglasses, the piano—the list is long.

Somehow the past still reflects well on modern Florentines. And yet their pride is no retrospective reaching after past glories. Nor does constant confrontation with their past produce an incipient inferiority complex. Rather, the past provides people with a powerful sense of their own identity, a sense of self-confidence borne of the knowledge that Florence—through good times and bad—has prospered for more than 2,000 years. And the reason it has prospered, of course, as any Florentine will tell you, is the Florentines themselves.

Culture and civilization Italians, albeit grudgingly, concede almost without exception that the Florentines are some of the most cultured and civilized people in Italy. Florentines are also hard working—not something Italians would say of the Romans or the Neapolitans, for example. They are also active and enterprising—witness the city's army of artisans—and, unlike the people of much of modern Italy, they still have a healthy respect for those who work the land (Tuscan peasants have long been considered the most intelligent of Italy's farmers). Yet for all their supposed pride, Florentines are also decorous and dignified people. And though individual in the extreme, they never cultivate the cult of the individual. Urbane, busy, cultured, and quietly self-satisfied—these are the Florentine watchwords.

> ❑ "The Florentines… invented the Renaissance, which is the same as saying they invented the modern world—not, of course, an unmitigated good."
> Mary McCarthy (1912–89) ❑

■ **Florence's wealth was founded on textiles and its artistic reputation on the sublimities of its Renaissance painters. No wonder, then, that cloth and the cult of the beautiful, together with the work of designers and craftspeople, continue to make Florence one of Italy's capitals of fashion and style ...■**

14

Good taste and high quality You have to look a long way in Italy to find a scruffy Italian. You have to look even farther in Florence, where old and young alike parade the city streets dressed as if preening on some vast outdoor catwalk. Nowhere, with the exception of Milan, is the art of the *bella figura*, of creating a good impression, more keenly practiced. Cool and intellectual, the Florentines look to subtle and sober-minded clothes, mixing tweedy English classicism with dashes of Renaissance opulence. On the business side, the city's textile barons favor quality. Artisans and upscale couturiers cohabit quite happily, weaving their magic from the most luxurious cloth, or conjuring up the jewelry and leatherware, for which the city is famous, from the most exclusive of materials.

Goodbye Gucci? Three big names roll off the tongue when talk in Florence turns to fashion. Biggest of all, though perhaps not the most fashionable, is Gucci, still based at Via de' Tornabuoni 73r where the firm was founded three generations ago. The company has been going through some difficult times, though the problems of widely available fakes and the excessive range of products that threatened to sink the firm have been fought off. In the wake of those difficulties came some bitter in fighting and a run-in with the U.S. and Italian

tax authorities. Where it counts, however, in the shop window, the company's leather goods—made from fine-quality, honey-cured hide—continue to appeal to those who covet the quiet panache of the famous "double G."

Emilio Pucci With his aristocratic bearing and ambassadorial aplomb, Il Marchese Emilio Pucci is the *doyen* of Florentine fashion, a popular society figure who often entertains visiting royalty and heads of state. He launched his fashion career in the 1950s with dramatically dyed silks—still fashionable today, when his company's design credentials extend to cars, perfume, and *objets d'art*. Pucci even dresses Florence's local

Emilio Pucci: high priest of Florentine fashion

> ❑ Machiavelli complained that the main preoccupations of Florentines were "to appear splendid in apparel and obtain a crafty shrewdness in discourse." ❑

Stepping out in style: hat, handbag, and all the trimmings

traffic police (the *vigili urbani*). In 1957, he launched his famous lingerie range—made from scraps of discarded silk. Unashamedly romantic, Pucci can also be refreshingly down to earth, once describing his fashion empire as a "modest endeavor in the rag trade."

Salvatore Ferragamo Born in Naples, Ferragamo emigrated to the United States when he was 15. He made his fortune in Hollywood, crafting shoes for the likes of Greta

Garbo, Vivien Leigh, Gloria Swanson, and the gladiators in Cecil B. de Mille costume epics. His spiritual home was really Florence, however, where his family still administers a fashion empire that now produces accessories and clothes to accompany the trademark shoes.

> ❑ The average Florentine spends something approaching a million lire annually on clothes. Some 10 per cent of Florence's income is generated by its fashion industry, whose main showcase is the famous trade fair, Pitti Moda, held in the Fortezza da Basso. ❑

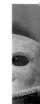

■ Sober and hardworking they may be, but Tuscans happily let the mask slip when it comes to celebration. Florence and Siena have the big set-piece festivals—Calcio in Costume, Maggio Musicale, and the Palio—but not even the smallest village lets the year go by without at least one excuse for riotous celebration ...■

Music and the arts Tuscans, and Florentines in particular, pride themselves on their culture. Colorful medieval memories may be evoked in their most famous pageants, but it is past glories of a cultural kind that they seek to celebrate in their more highbrow arts festivals.
Performances of music, dance, and drama are held throughout the

Poster for a Saracen joust

region, often in magnificent medieval settings or, as in the case of Fiesole, in outdoor theaters of Roman vintage. Concert series fill Florentine churches, and they are also presented in green secluded corners (as in Barga's famous opera festival). Some festivals, such as San Gimignano's, are provincial affairs confined to the town square. Others, such as Florence's Maggio Musicale (see

❑ Art and music festivals in Tuscany include the following:
Arezzo Choral music (late August)
Barga Opera and theater (late July)
Fiesole Estate Fiesolana—music, film, ballet, and drama (June–August)
Florence Maggio Musicale—orchestral concerts, ballet, movies, and fringe events (April–June)
Lucca Sacred music (April–June)
Montepulciano Cantiere Internazionale—music and arts (end July/beginning August)
Siena Settimana Musicale—concerts by pupils and staff of the Accademia Musicale Chigiana (August)
Torre del Lago Puccini operas performed outdoors (August) ❑

page 183), are among Italy's most popular and prestigious arts events. Visit any Tuscan tourist office for details of current festivals.

Food and wine It need not be much —an obscure saint, the humble potato—anything will do as long as it provides an excuse for a party. Small *feste* or *sagre* erupt across Tuscany throughout the year. Most take place in the summer, when long balmy evenings provide the perfect background for a night of festivities. Autumn, however, will do just as well, for then the grapes are brought in, and what better reason for celebration than a good harvest? Most village festivals begin with a special Mass, followed by much dancing, overindulgence (of food rather than

16

drink) and a rousing fireworks finale. Brass bands provide a musical accompaniment (often of excruciating quality but quite remarkable enthusiasm). You should stumble across many such festivals by accident. If not, they are widely advertised on street posters and in local newspapers.

Medieval echoes Italians love nothing more than spectacle and sensuality. Siena's famous Palio (see pages 240–1), therefore, like many similar pageants, may seem to be little more than an excuse to dress up and indulge in days of rampant (but motiveless) merrymaking. To the cynical, such festivities can also appear like attempts to woo the wealthy tourist. Nothing, however, could be further from the truth. Many such events recall ancient but still passionately felt enmities (Siena's Palio, with its inter district rivalries, is a perfect example). Most are means of expressing fiercely felt civic pride. Some, like Florence's Scoppio del Carro (see page 75), wear a spurious religious mantle—often no more than a mask for an event whose origins have pagan roots. The majority revel in competition, usually between neighboring districts. Encounters can range from the ferocious—as in Siena's horserace—to the faintly ridiculous, as in Montepulciano's comical barrel-rolling contest, the

❏ Among the more entertaining traditional festivals are:
Arezzo Giostro del Saracino (September)
Florence Scoppio del Carro (Easter Sunday); Festa di San Giovanni (June); Calcio in Costume (June); Festa del Grillo (August 15); Festa del Rificolone (September 7)
Lucca San Paolino (July); Luminara (September 13); Santa Croce (September 14)
Montepulciano Bravio delle Botti (August)
Pisa Luminara & Regatta di San Ranieri (June); Gioco del Ponte (June)
Pistoia Giostro dell'Orso (July)
Prato Festa degli Omaggi (September)
Siena Palio (July 2 and August 16) ❏

Bravio delle Botti (see page 215). Ludicrous or not, the stakes are always high, the battles furiously contested. For example, Florence's Calcio in Costume—a mass game of soccer in medieval dress—involves bruising passages of play and a medley of viciously underhanded tactics.

The Campo in Siena during the Palio, Italy's most famous pageant

■ **Old traditions of craft and artistic endeavor die hard. Florence's modern artisans, worthy successors to their Renaissance forebears, are still part of the city's mythology, whether carving furniture in dusty workshops or crafting jewelry in the venerable environs of the Ponte Vecchio ...■**

Craft on every corner Few modern cities would find a place in their hard-pressed hearts for a breed straight out of the Middle Ages. In Florence, however, artisans (*artigiani*) are very much a part of life. Although rising rents have driven craftsmen out of some central districts, other areas buzz with skilled activity. On Via della Porcellana, for example, near Ognissanti, every doorway is a tumult of chair legs and dismembered tables, every interior a vignette of wood shavings and leather-aproned carpenters. A similar scene greets you around Santa Croce, where the smell of wood glue fills your nostrils and the clank of wrought iron rends the air. The picture is repeated (though in a different guise) on the Ponte Vecchio, where you can look over the shoulders of latter-day portrait painters as they flatter their eager clients. Around them, as likely as not, will be the wares of less subtle deceivers—the fake Chanel bags and Gucci watches of less reputable artisans, tucked away in more discreet workshops. Shops on the bridge itself are packed with glittering jewelry, the work of skilled successors to Renaissance goldsmiths such as Ghiberti and Benvenuto Cellini. Nowhere is the lack of distinction between artist and artisan more apparent than in Florence.

Continue beyond the bridge into the Oltrarno and you enter another artisans' heartland. While fine antique shops front the thorough-fares, small ateliers jam the back-streets, home to leather workshops (that of Santo Spirito the most famous) and some of the city's longest-established cabinetmakers. If their wares prove too expensive, visit

Artisans are still an integral and important feature of the city

the market around San Lorenzo for a huge choice of leather and clothing. If not, broaden your scope by visiting the stores on Via de' Tornabuoni, a shop window for the city's finest craftsmanship (see Shopping, pages 178–81, for details).

Tradition Artisans provide a living reminder of the past in a city whose history otherwise seems confined to museums and galleries. Not only in their workshops (whose appearance has probably changed little in five centuries) but also in the crafts they carry out, these workers continue to provide a glimpse of a lost world. They may not produce paintings of Renaissance caliber, but in virtually all other areas their skills are as sharply honed as ever. The variety of craftspeople, too, is as broad as ever: from frame makers, ceramicists, stonecutters, and jewelers, to furniture makers, silversmiths, weavers, and textile designers.

Pressed into service At no time was the strength of the city's craft tradition more dramatically revealed, nor more desperately needed, than in the aftermath of the 1966 flood. Dozens of skills old and new had to be found to deal with the deluge of damaged artifacts. Many ancient crafts had to be revived (notably the art of illuminating manuscripts); others were virtually unknown (such as the restoration of paper). For the most part, however, the city was able to draw on talent still latent in its thriving artistic subculture.

The Opificio delle Pietre Dure provides an excellent example of tradition merging with modern techniques in the service of art. Founded

In the shadow of the Uffizi gallery, local artists look for work

in 1588, the institute started life making mosaics from *pietre dure* (literally "hard stone")—usually semi-precious stones like agate and amethyst. The epitome of its work is found in the Medici Chapels' Cappella dei Principi (see pages 64–5). These days its teaching departments and modern laboratories are world leaders in restoration of all kinds, drawing from the craftspeople of Florence not only for *pietre dure* specialists, but also for experts in furniture, painting, stone, marble, bronze, and textiles.

■ **Good food is as much a part of the pleasure of a holiday in Florence and Tuscany as visiting the region's museums and art galleries. Eating out in a wayside trattoria or a downtown restaurant should provide a medley of memories every bit as satisfying as a Donatello nude or a Masaccio fresco ...■**

Florence and French cuisine

Florentines never tire of telling visitors how they invented French cuisine. In 1533, so the story goes, Caterina de' Medici, aged just 14, married Henri de Valois, later to become Henri II of France. Loath (like any good Italian) to leave the joys of home cooking, and appalled by the prospect of foreign food and French table manners, the young Caterina ensured that a train of chefs and an encyclopedia of recipes followed her to Paris. Hence, supposedly, the range of classic Gallic dishes with

Mushrooms are a specialty of the region in the autumn

more than a hint of Tuscan seasoning: *dolce forte* (from *lepre dolce e forte*); *canard à l'orange* (Tuscany's *papero alla melarancia*); and *vol au vents* (sold in Florentine *pasticcerie* as *turbanate di sfoglia*). Caterina is also supposed to have introduced the French to that most vital piece of table equipment, the fork.

Rich repasts Whatever the truth of the story, medieval Tuscan meals, at least on big occasions, were far richer than the simple dishes that make up today's regional cuisine. The banquets of Pope Leo X, the Medici pope, for example, featured delicacies such as peacocks' tongues, and spectacles such as nightingales flying out of pies and children springing naked from puddings. At the other extreme, poor Florentines might sup on little more than dried figs and oak-bark bread. The average family, by contrast, would settle down to something resembling a modern meal—wine, pasta, ravioli, sausage and grilled meat, and fruit or cheese to finish. Medieval flavorings, however, would raise eyebrows in a modern kitchen. Soups, for example, might have been seasoned with cloves, cinnamon, and ginger, and garnished with sugar, cheese, and almonds. Pies overflowed with oil, orange and lemon juice, cloves, nutmeg, parsley, saffron, dates, raisins, bay leaves, and marjoram. One sauce, *savore sanguino*, boasted cinnamon, raisins, sandalwood, and sumac, the last now used only for tanning leather.

Today's temptations You would be hard pressed to find anything as exotic in today's restaurants. Quite

the contrary: Florentines—wrongly—are now known for their culinary parsimony, and are labeled by other Italians as mere *mangiafagioli* (bean eaters). Beans, in many forms, certainly feature in many Florentine dishes, but they are symbols rather than staples of the city's healthily robust cuisine. There is much else to appeal, from warming Tuscan vegetable soups like *ribollita* and *acqua-cotta*, to that mother of all steaks, the hearty *bistecca alla fiorentina*. Fruit and vegetables, locally grown and market-bought, are superb, and in season there are such delights as truffles and *porcini* mushrooms to tempt the taste buds.

As in Rome, which loves its brains and offal dishes, Florence can also taunt the palate with specialties that some might consider a little beyond the culinary pale. Tripe and pigs' intestines (*lampredotto*) are two

❏ Downtown restaurants run the gamut, from expensive post-modern to tatty *trattorie*. The areas around Santo Spirito (in Oltrarno) and Santa Croce are rewarding, with many small, interesting restaurants. Cheap pizzerias and lively *osterie* cluster around the station and Santa Maria Novella. ❏

classic dishes, as are the combs, livers, hearts, and testicles of freshly killed roosters. You may wish to pass over such delicacies, but do try to move beyond staples like spaghetti and tomato sauce to sample some of Florence's more interesting special-ties (see also pages 210–11).

A tempting sight—take your pick of the city's trattorie

■ **No one pretends that Florentines revel in the *dolce vita* to the extent of their Roman counterparts. With a café on every corner, however, and a summer sun overhead, opportunities for the *dolce far niente*—the sweet doing of nothing—are as rich in Florence as almost anywhere in Italy ...■**

Time out The simple pleasures of a quiet *cappuccino*, or a calming *aperitivo*, are as much a part of enjoying Italy as trudging around museums and galleries (and this is as true for a native as it is for a foreigner). No self-respecting Italian city, therefore, can do without its bars and cafés. And while Florence's streets and piazzas may seem less welcoming than some, they still provide a colorful and more than adequate stage for lazy self-indulgence. They also provide the wherewithal for that other passive pastime—people-watching.

Cafés are there to be used—and not merely as pit stops for a gulp of coffee before another round of Giotto and Michelangelo. After hours of paintings and sculpture, of churches dutifully seen, treat yourself to an hour or two of more

❏ Florence's best-known cafés are the "Big Four" on Piazza della Repubblica: **Donnini** (excellent coffee and cakes), **Paszkowski** (literary associations, music on the terrace summer evenings), **Giubbe Rosse** (peruse the daily papers with your coffee), and (best of them all, one-time haunt of the intelligentsia) the *belle-époque* **Gilli**. ❏

wholehearted self-indulgence. Such simple delights may be denied you on your return to daily routines.

A choice of styles There is a bar on almost every Florentine street corner—functional, stand-up places designed for a kick-start *espresso*, a breakfast *cornetto* (a horn-shaped, custard-filled croissant), or a hurried lunchtime snack. All human life is here, together with all it needs to keep body and soul together. Bars are shops, pubs, phone booths, and social meeting places rolled into one.

Cafés are a little different. You can still stand and fight for service, but more often than not they provide oases of leisurely and sun-drenched contemplation. Relaxation, not to mention waiter service, comes at a price (you pay extra to sit down), but even the most humble purchase buys the right to read, daydream, or simply get your bearings for as long as you wish.

Service with a smile

A slightly different experience awaits in the city's wine cellars, old-fashioned institutions that parade under a variety of names—*vinaio*, *fiaschetteria*, *mescita*. Some, like the *Cantinetta Antinori* (in Piazza Antinori), are stylish, rather upscale affairs. Others, like the hole-in-the-wall *Vini del Chianti* (Via dei Cimatori), are more modest neighborhood joints. Most offer places to meet for a chat and a bite to eat (with, of course, a glass or two of wine).

People-watching There comes a time—when the postcards are written and you are dead on your feet—when the world has to come to you. Then is the moment to forget the galleries, ignore the churches, and sit back, drink in hand, to watch the Italians and your fellow travelers at play. People-watching in Italy is a rare delight. No time is better to indulge in it than during the social ritual known as the *passeggiata*, a stylized evening parade when the object is to

Taking time, with a cup of coffee, to catch up on the news

dress up and then to see and be seen (in Florence its ebb and flow centers on Piazza della Signoria and the streets around Via dei Calzaiuoli). Traffic and narrow streets preclude ranks of Parisian-style boulevard cafés (premium spots for the amateur voyeur): in Florence, the most famous cafés crowd Piazza della Signoria or the more dour margins of Piazza della Repubblica. Many equally picturesque spots —with a more "local" feel—await discovery in the quieter corners of the Oltrarno.

❏ The expensive but essential **Rivoire** on Piazza della Signoria is one of Florence's most famous cafés, perfect for admiring the clothes-conscious Italians carrying out their evening *passeggiata*. ❏

■ **Tourism in any great city is invariably a double-edged blessing. On the one hand it offers revenue and employment, on the other it encourages the less scrupulous and adds to the wear and tear on the very monuments visitors come to see. Restoration, as a result, is a constant Florentine preoccupation. Today more than ever, the city is struggling to maintain a balance between protecting the legacy of its illustrious past and carving for itself a realistic and economically sound future ...■**

Too many tourists Estimates vary as to how many people visit Florence every year. The evidence of one's own eyes, however, suggests it is too many. It is as well, therefore, to come expecting to share the city's attractions with a great many other people: prepared for the crowds forever clustered around the Uffizi's Botticellis, and for the numbers of young visitors of many countries sprawled around the Duomo and the Ponte Vecchio.

Overcrowding is a problem that touches the Florentine at least as much as the harassed tourist. Those who live in Florence are the ones, day in, day out, who bear the intolerable strain visitors place on the city's infrastructure—though they are also, of course, the ones who reap tourism's financial benefits. Visitors, however, can only be partly blamed for the city's traffic, a daily threat to life and limb (quite apart from the effects of vehicle-induced pollution on the health of statues and stonework). Here locals are their own worst enemies: there are, on average, 2.7 cars for every Florentine family. And cars—with food, family, and soccer—are the things closest to an Italian's heart. Getting rid of them, therefore, has been an uphill battle: downtown restrictions were introduced only in 1988, and then only after considerable argument.

Florence fossilized? Florentines are currently faced with a difficult choice: whether to go for broke (perhaps literally as well as metaphorically) and retain Florence as a living city, or whether to turn it over entirely to the demands of tourism. If they tend toward the latter, Florence may be in danger of becoming a historical fossil, a moribund city dressed up as a Renaissance theme park. Death by tourism can be brought on by a variety of causes. They include slow strangulation by traffic, paralysis by depopulation, food shops replaced by souvenir stands, workshops replaced by boutiques, neighborhood *trattorie* sacrificed to the gods of fast food.

The problem echoes that of Venice, whose population has dropped to 70,000 today from 180,000 in 1945. Florentine figures show a similar trend, down from 400,000 before the 1966 flood to an estimated 150,000 today. But for Florence, such discouraging statistics are generally tempered by glimmers of optimism.

Firenze Nuova One much-heralded way forward for Florence is the new town on the city's northwestern outskirts, around the airport. Firenze Nuova, so the theory goes, will encourage urban decentralization and create the focus for a broad-based industrial and municipal metropolis, its economy increasingly intertwined with that of its booming neighbor, Prato. Florence itself, the planners hope, will increasingly be freed to develop as a culture- and service-oriented city. Critics (of which, as ever in Italy, there are many) complain that the scheme could have the opposite effect, creating a desiccated

downtown on the one hand, and a steel and glass wasteland on the other. So far, the critics appear to have been confounded: many of the traditional businesses, such as banking, publishing, architecture, and legal services, seem likely to remain in central Florence. Many Florentine professionals perhaps prefer the more stimulating environment of the city itself, with its Renaissance palaces and statues, and have no intention of surrendering Florence to tourism.

Crime Whatever the impression given by the city's urbane citizens and benign-looking streets, all is not well below the surface. Florentines talk of *Firenze snaturata* (Florence corrupted), a phrase used to describe both the threat of the city's surrender to tourists and its growing catalog of crime. Prostitution and drug dealing are mainstays of the Florentine underworld, just as in many cities in the 1990s. It can be hard not to notice the drug deals on Via de' Neri, or the late-night lowlife cluttered around the station and the Cascine park, proving that there is more to the city than statues and sweet-

The volume of visitors (top, Uffizi and below, Piazza SS Annunziata) increases wear on the monuments

Making friends with the Porcellino near the Mercato Nuovo

Orsanmichele's exterior statues, removed—like the Campanile's corroded reliefs and Michelangelo's *David*—to the pollution-free sanctuary of museums and galleries.

The unending task of restoring works of art damaged by time and pollution is one thing; repairing the damage done in a mere few hours by the 1966 flood is quite another. The deluge created one of the greatest artistic (and human) disasters in Italy's recent history (see pages 130–1). Some of the thousands of damaged artworks were lost forever and many are still waiting to see the light of day. Most, however, were restored, almost miraculously in many cases, testament to the dedication and technical skills of Florence's restorers.

The sheer size of Italy's artistic heritage means that funds for restoration are constantly at a premium. After the 1966 flood, however, huge additional sums of money were donated to Florence. Much of the money is still being put to good use in a massive restoration project that is destined to last another 20 years.

Not all the city's restoration projects have been without incident. Piazza della Signoria provided the worst recent upheaval: excavations turned the square into a construction site, then the original medieval paving stones were mysteriously "lost." The pedestrianization scheme (the *Zona Blu*) has also been a mixed success. It is, however, typical of the projects increasingly needed by a city struggling to reconcile two disparate sets of demands—the requirements of visitors seeking its Renaissance past and the needs of citizens looking to its 21st-century future.

faced gallery Madonnas. However, this is not to say that Florence is particularly dangerous, nor is it plagued with the petty crime of, say, Rome or Naples. Pickpockets aside, the city's criminal element is unlikely to affect most reasonably vigilant visitors.

Pollution and restoration Still on the down side, but again in common with cities the world over, air pollution is an increasing worry in Florence. It is true that the city has some way to go before it faces the pollution problems of Rome or Milan. Nonetheless, the danger signs are already there, and are of special concern in a city that has more than its share of outdoor art treasures. The begrimed Battistero is a prominent victim, its bronze doors now removed from their proximity to belching exhausts and replaced by copies. Gone, too, are most of

---

❑ Over 30 years after the 1966 flood, some 80 full-time staff are still employed restoring books and manuscripts in the National Library, where more than a million volumes were ruined. About 2,000 of the 3,000 paintings and sculptures dredged from the mud have so far been returned to public view. ❑

FLORENCE WAS

■ Although Florence was a late arrival on the historical stage—only six decades before the birth of Christ—its beginnings have become entangled in a heady mix of myth and countermyth. Even the origins of its name are obscured by an opaque combination of fact and fantasy ...■

28

The Etruscans Florence was probably first inhabited by Italic tribes from latter-day Emilia-Romagna around the end of the 10th century BC. The main attraction of the site was simple: it provided a crossing point over the Arno, one of the region's more formidable natural barriers (the ford was close to the site of the present-day Ponte Vecchio). When the Etruscans drifted into the area five centuries later, however (see pages 246–7), they ignored the river in favor of a more easily defended position in the hills to the north. In time their craggy fortress became

Fiesole (see pages 82–3), a colony that developed into a leading member of the Etruscans' 12-city federation. At the same time, the Etruscans probably kept a small market on the Arno, and a breakaway group from Fiesole may also have established a community near the river in the 4th century BC.

The end of Fiesole By this time, Rome was rapidly encroaching on the Etruscan dominions. Fiesole was first defeated in 283 BC, but it continued, like many Etruscan cities, to enjoy a relationship of benevolent neutrality with the ever more powerful city of Rome. Fiesole's end, according to legend, came around 60 BC, when Rome sent an expedition to hunt down Catiline, a fugitive from Roman justice. Catiline, it seems, had fled to Fiesole and assumed control of the city (to the delight of its inhabitants). Fiorino, commander of the Roman forces, realizing Fiesole was powerfully defended, decided to build a camp on the Arno and take the city by siege. Killed in a surprise raid, however, his plans came to nothing, but his successor, Julius Caesar, consolidated the riverside camp and eventually defeated Fiesole. As for Catiline, he escaped, only to be hunted down and killed near Pistoia.

Fact and fiction Most of this colorful account is pure fiction—and with it the notion that Florence took its name (and owed its existence) to the slain commander, Fiorino. Catiline

Etruscan art: (top) black figure vase and (left) funerary urn from Chiusi

was a historical figure, *was* in Fiesole, and *was* defeated at Pistoia in 62 BC. Fiorino, however, seems to be an entirely literary invention. Julius Caesar probably never fought in Tuscany; nor did he found Roman Florentia (though he is often described as doing so). His role in the city's birth was passive. It was his agrarian law of 59 BC that—by making provision for land to be granted to retired army veterans—actually created the conditions for Florence's establishment and early growth.

The name of Florence How Florence came by its romantic name is a mystery. Many would still like to believe it was named after Fiorino and his fictitious camp (and, though history is silent on the subject, there may well have been such a general in Caesar's army). Others think it derives from *fluentia*, after the fact that the Arno "flows" through the city (though plenty of rivers flow through cities).

Wandering among the ruins of Fiesole, Florence's Etruscan predecessor in the hills above the Arno

Another theory, along similar lines, suggests that *fluentia* refers to the "confluence" of the Arno and Mugnone (the river that joins the Arno about a mile west of the city).

Popular tradition, however, favors more poetic semantic possibilities—centering on Florence as a "city of flowers" (*fiori*). Roman Florentia, for example, might have taken its name from the wildflowers that dot the city's hills and plains. Or it may have derived from the Ludi Floreales, a program of spring games held to honor the goddess Flora. The city's cathedral is still known as Santa Maria del Fiore, after the *giaggiolo*, or *Iris florentia*, the violet-scented iris of the Florentine hills. The purple flower (shaped like a fleur-de-lis) is also the city's emblem and the symbol of the Virgin Mary.

■ **Under Roman domination, Florence enjoyed a period of quiet prosperity. After Rome's fall the city took the barbarian invasions more or less in its stride. Lombard and Carolingian rule then laid the foundations of an independent city, and with it the prospect of Florence's medieval power and prosperity ...■**

30

A Roman city Florence's Roman stalwarts established a walled *castrum*, a camp whose grid outline is still clearly imprinted on the city's present-day streets. Its northern and southern limits, for example, are marked by Via de' Cerretani and Via Porta Rossa, its eastern and western boundaries by Via del Proconsolo and Via de' Tornabuoni. Piazza della Repubblica was the old Forum, Via degli Strozzi its main street (the *Decumanus Maximus*). The old theater lay behind the Palazzo Vecchio, the amphitheater within the curve of Via Torta and Piazza dei Peruzzi (near Santa Croce).

Today, only a few columns remain as direct memorials of the colony of Florentia. Some are in the church of San Miniato al Monte, others form part of the Battistero, site of the Roman *praetorium* or guardhouse (and possibly the Roman governor's residence). Otherwise, monuments amount to no more than historical

echoes, vague memories recalled by street names such as Via delle Terme (Street of the Baths) or Via del Campidoglio (Street of the Capitol).

Decline and fall Florence's main role under the Romans was strategic. Florentia not only provided a route over the Arno, but also controlled the passes across the Apennines into Emilia-Romagna. Although the settlement's first walls took no account of the Arno, it was the river—navigable to this point—that provided a conduit for trade and generated the colony's early prosperity. Consular roads, too, made the camp their focus, notably the Via Cassia, a link between Rome and its big colonies at Bononia (Bologna) and Mediolanum (Milan). The Via Aurelia, the Via Clodia, and

Top: the façade on the Roman villa at Poggio a Chiano. Below: the great Roman theater at Fiesole

the Via Flaminia—built before Florentia's rise—also crisscrossed the region, further emphasizing the new colony's strategic importance. Although Florentia was never a major player in the Roman world, by around the 3rd century AD (after expansion during the Augustan period) the city's population had probably reached about 10,000.

The Barbarians After Rome's fall, Florence suffered repeated attacks from Goth and Byzantine invaders. Ultimately, however, it was the Lombards, a Germanic people from the north, who dominated the city during the Dark Ages. After taking Tuscany in AD 570, they brought two centuries of relative peace to the troubled region, which they administered from Pavia and Lucca. Their reign was cut short by the Franks (another northern race), first under Pepin the Short, and then under his more famous son, Charlemagne, who probably visited the city on a couple of occasions. Tuscany became part of the Franks' Carolingian Empire (later the Holy Roman Empire), ruled on behalf of its northern emperors by a series of Lucca-based princes known as the Margraves.

The rule of the Margraves The Carolingian empire's hold over the Margraves grew progressively weaker. As it waned, the Margraves were becoming increasingly fond of Florence. Willa, widow of the Margrave Uberto, for example, founded the Badia Fiorentina, the city's first abbey (see page 55), in 978. By 1001 Willa's son, the Margrave Ugo, transferred the

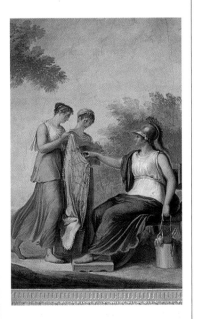

Rome continued to influence the art of Tuscany long after the fall of the empire

region's capital from Lucca to Florence. Thereafter, Margrave allegiance to northern-based emperors slackened still further. By 1077 the pious Margrave Matilda (1046–1115), founder of many churches and one of the era's most successful rulers, had transferred her loyalties to the pope (by now already involved in virulent disputes with the emperor—see pages 36–7). At her death she bequeathed her titles to Pope Gregory VII—all, that is, except Lucca, Florence, and Siena, all three of which found themselves on the verge of independence and self-determination.

31

■ **The medieval prosperity of Florence was based on Europe's greatest woolen and textiles industry. This enterprise in turn nurtured a banking system whose success laid the foundations of modern capitalism and made Florentines bankers to much of the known world ...**■

Early success At its peak, the textiles industry in Florence employed an estimated 30,000 people—about one third of the city's population. During the 12th century, barely 100 years after the trade began, some 300 textile workshops were scattered across the city. Even by the end of the 13th century, when production had dropped by almost 90 per cent, Florence still provided the Western world with at least one tenth of its textiles.

There were several reasons for Florence's success. One was water, fundamental to the woolen industry (both sorted wool and finished cloth, for example, had to be washed and rinsed). In the Arno, therefore, the city had a primary resource. Another was the availability of expertise and cheap labor. The expertise was provided by the Umiliati, a group of monks introduced to the city from Lombardy. Their riverside workshops made Ognissanti (see page 109) one of the industry's main centers. They helped train the city's teeming ranks of carders, combers, weavers, shearers, spinners, and other specialized artisans. Money, too, was of prime

Top: detail, Villa Medicea Poggio a Caiano. Below: an eagle, symbol of the Arte di Calimala, crowns San Miniato al Monte

importance, and here Florence's bankers came into their own, providing the industry with capital investment and extended lines of credit.

Florence was also renowned for the quality of its cloth. Its reputation for dyeing, in particular, was second to none. Exotic dyestuffs came from every corner of the Orient and the Mediterranean basin, Florentine reds becoming particularly prized (many of the dyers' secrets, incidentally, are now lost—one of history's more tantalizing mysteries). All Florence lacked was wool. This problem was solved by the city's enterprising merchants who—"in the name of God and profit"—traveled to England, Portugal, Spain, Flanders, and the Barbary Coast to buy raw materials to feed their flourishing businesses.

Europe's bankers Florentine bankers championed the use of bills of exchange, and invented checks, credit, life insurance, double-entry bookkeeping, and Europe's first single currency, the gold florin. On their own these might seem dry achievements. In the context of what a banker might do with his profits, however, they provided the financial wherewithal for

many of the greatest buildings and works of art of the Renaissance.

The best known of the bankers, of course, were the Medici, whose bank, in its day, was Europe's single wealthiest business. A 15th-century phenomenon, the family were late-comers to an industry that by 1250 already dominated the world of European commerce. The Bardi and the Peruzzi, for example, were chief bankers to the kings of England and France; the Acciaiuoli dealt with the Angevin monarchs of Naples and Sicily; while the Pazzi, the Alberti (and the Medici) handled the highly lucrative papal account. Lesser financiers from among Florence's 24 banking dynasties—involved with Holy Roman emperors, German potentates, and Burgundian princes—are remembered today in the city's palaces and street names—Alberti, Albizzi, Antinori, Capponi, Cerchi, Davanzati, Guardi, Mozzi, Portinari, Ricci, Strozzi, and Tornabuoni.

The florin One of the bankers' key achievements was the *fiorino d'oro* (gold florin), a coin which was adopted across Europe after its introduction in 1252, and which remained in use until the middle of the 15th cen-

Top and above: details, the Palazzo dell'Arte della Lana

tury. Florentines had previously used the *mark*, minted in Pisa, while the only internationally accepted coin had been the Byzantine *hyperper*. (The English florin, whose name survived in British coinage until recently, took its name from the *fiorino*.) Purity was vital to the coin's stability, and standards at the Zecca (Mint), alongside the Palazzo Vecchio, were rigorously applied. By 1422, 2 million *fiorini* were in circulation. One side bore a likeness of John the Baptist, Florence's patron saint; the other was inscribed with the city's Latin name, Florentia, and its floral emblem.

❑ In the 1430s, a family could live comfortably on 150 florins a year; a *palazzo* could be bought for 1,000, a Botticelli painting for 100, a slave for 50, and a servant for 10. The Medici accounts for the years 1433–71 showed 663,755 florins spent over 38 years on "buildings, charities, and taxes." ❑

■ **The city's great mercantile endeavors were organized into *Arti* (Guilds). Their leading lights were invariably to be found either running the city as officeholders in the official machinery of government, or manipulating affairs more subtly through their position at the head of its supposedly independent institutions ...■**

34

A society of merchants As early as the 11th century, Florentine merchants organized themselves into a *societas mercatorum.* Ranged against them was the *societas militium,* a grouping of nobles and leading Florentine families. The former provided the backbone of the *comune,* the independent city-state, run by a 100-strong assembly and established in Florence after Margrave Matilda's death in 1115. In time, the *societas* was replaced by the first of the guilds, the Arte di Calimala, an umbrella organization devoted to most mercantile vocations. By the end of the 12th century, however, splinter groups had broken away to form seven major guilds, the Arti Maggiori.

The Arti Maggiori The most prestigious of the guilds, though not the wealthiest, was the lawyers' Arte dei Giudici e Notai. Next came the wool, silk, and cloth merchants—the Arte della Lana, the Arte di Por Santa Maria, and the refashioned Arte di Calimala. Lower down came the Arte del Cambio, or bankers' guild (bankers preferred the term "money-changers," usury being a sin in the eyes of the Church). The Arte dei Vaccai e Pellicciai looked after the furriers. The Arte dei Medici, Speziali e Merciai embraced a hodgepodge of doctors, apothecaries, and spice- and dye-merchants (as well as the occasional poet, painter, and craftsman).

The Arti Minori While the Arti Maggiori embraced wealthy merchants, the 14 minor guilds (founded in 1289) catered more to middle-ranking tradesmen. These included anyone from butchers, bakers, and armorers to carpenters, masons, and innkeepers (not to mention vintners, tanners, cooks, locksmiths, and leather workers). Ordinary workers, however, the so-called *Popolo Minuto,* had no representation at all—despite making up 75 per cent of the population. Those employed in the wool, silk, and cloth industries, moreover, were prevented by law from forming guilds.

The power of the merchant class Merchants, known as the *Popolo Grasso* (literally the "fat people"), controlled Florence during much of the 13th and 14th centuries. Sometimes the control was covert, at other times plain to see, as in the so-called Primo Popolo (1248), a quasi-democratic regime dominated by mercantile elements (whose 10-year rule, according to Dante, was the only period of civic peace in Florence's history). During the Secondo Popolo (1284), the Arti Maggiori introduced the *Ordinamenti della Giustizia* (1293), a written constitution that, while theoretically the blueprint for republican rule, in fact entrenched mercantile power still further.

Government by guilds Florence's much-vaunted republicanism worked well in theory. The names of selected guild members (and only guild members) were placed in eight leather bags (*borse*) kept in Santa Croce. Names were then drawn at random in public. Those selected were known as *Priori,* the government they formed the *Signoria.* There were usually nine *Priori,* six chosen from the Arti Maggiori, two from the Arti Minori, and one standard-bearer, the

Gonfaloniere. The *Priori* served a maximum term of office of two months—a deliberately short period, in order to reduce the chances of corruption or favoritism. In times of crisis a *Parlemento*, or assembly, was summoned, consisting of all male citizens over the age of 14. When a two-thirds quorum was reached, the *Parlemento* was asked to approve a *balia*, a committee delegated to deal with the crisis as it saw fit.

Florence's republican system looked good on paper. In practice it was far from democratic. The lowliest workers, the *Popolo Minuto*, were totally excluded, as were the *grandi*, or nobles. Despite the random selection process, merchant cliques easily ensured that only the names of likely supporters found their way into the *borse*. If things did not go their way, it was easy enough to summon a *Parlemento* and form a *balia* whose first act would be to replace the offending *Priori* with more pliable candidates. It was thus, through the long decades of Medici rule, that the family retained the reins of power while only rarely holding formal office.

Top: sails, symbol of the Rucellai family, S. Maria Novella. Below: patron saints of the major guilds decorate Orsanmichele's exterior

■ **Florence was torn by internal disputes throughout the medieval period. Matters came to a head during the 13th century with the so-called Guelph–Ghibelline conflicts. Ostensibly encounters between papal and imperial supporters, these divisions were often no more than labels for any number of different feuds and factions ...■**

Endless enmity There has hardly been a time in Florence's 2,000-year history when the city was not divided into two or more rival camps. Dante compared its constant political struggles to a sick man forever tossing and turning in bed. So unending was the discord that contemporaries believed two different races had settled Florence: the nobles, descended from Roman soldiers, and the commoners, descendants of Fiesole's ancient Etruscans. Trying to follow

Emperor Barbarossa—"Red Beard" —and (top) his court at Mayence

the city's litany of feuds is pointless—and makes monotonous reading. All one can do is trace the main divisions, and remember that, for all the apparent conflict, Florence went from strength to strength.

Pope versus emperor The Guelphs and the Ghibellines took their names from "Welf"—the family name of Otto IV and the dukes of Bavaria— and "Waiblingen"—the name of a castle belonging to their rivals, the imperial family of Hohenstaufen. The Guelphs, broadly speaking, were supporters of the pope, the Ghibellines supporters of the Holy Roman Emperor. Disputes between emperor and pope dated back to the investiture of Charlemagne, who had given lands conquered in Italy to the papacy (the beginnings of the Papal States). In return he had been anointed and crowned Holy Roman Emperor. This was the root of irreconcilable differences: the popes claimed the right to crown emperors; the emperors claimed the right to sanction popes. Even more importantly, both parties claimed the right to rule the lands that made up the ancient Roman empire: the pope argued that Constantine the Great had bequeathed the empire to the Church, while the emperor cited lineal descent from the Roman and Byzantine emperors.

The dispute first came to a head in 1079 when Emperor Henry IV rejected Pope Gregory VII's proposals for radical reform (aimed at securing exclusive papal powers to control the selection and investiture of bishops). Gregory responded by excommunicating the emperor, in theory thereby freeing his subjects from imperial

allegiance. While diplomacy eventually settled this dispute (in the Concordat of Worms), subsequent disagreements were to involve violent confrontations on Italian soil, the most notorious of which was Emperor Barbarossa's 12th-century rampage to restore imperial authority.

Flags of convenience Conflicts within Italy's city-states, including Florence, rarely divided along simple Guelph–Ghibelline lines. By the time the words entered the language (in the 12th century) they were little more than convenient labels for a variety of feuding factions. Cities used alliances with pope or emperor, for example, as means to their own ends, the terms "Guelph" and "Ghibelline" serving as mere window dressing for squabbles between cities, or feuds between families within cities. If your sympathies were broadly Guelph (like those of Florence), the chances are your neighbor (and enemy) would be nominally Ghibelline (like Siena).

Florence divided The main division among the citizens of Florence was between the old nobility, who had Ghibelline sympathies, and the new class of entrepreneurs, who were Guelphs. By 1193, the infighting was so disruptive that the *Comune* introduced political refinements such as the post of *Podestà* (a chief magistrate) to help defuse the situation

The Bargello's courtyard, scene of countless executions during the Guelph and Ghibelline conflicts

(see pages 56, 57). In 1216, in one famous incident, street battles were triggered by the murder of one Buondelmonti, stabbed for reneging on a promise to marry a member of the Amidei family. (This was the supposed spark of Florence's Guelph–Ghibelline conflicts.) Although Ghibelline regimes reigned briefly (in both 1237 and 1260), Florence was predominantly a Guelph (mercantile) city—though, in keeping with the divisive spirit of the times, the Guelphs themselves managed to quarrel and split into two factions—the Whites and the Blacks (see page 71).

Civil chaos in most cities of the period invariably had the same outcome—the emergence of a single man or family with the wealth and power to cut through the tangle of feuding and factionalism. It was only a matter of time before just such a family emerged in Florence.

❏ "Nearly every form of government was tried … in Florence," but Florentines were "too articulate, politically, for government to be possible at all." Mary McCarthy (1912–89) ❏

■ Few families' names are more associated with a city than that of the Medici with Florence. The phenomenal wealth of their banking business sustained them as the city's virtual rulers for 350 years. During this period, Medici patronage produced some of the greatest buildings and works of art ever seen ...■

Giovanni di Bicci de' Medici (1360–1429), founder of the Medici banking business in the late 14th century, could scarcely have predicted that his descendants would rule Florence until 1737, that they would include popes and cardinals, and that they would marry into the noble families of Spain and Austria, providing spouses for such illustrious names as Charles I of England, Philip II of Spain, Philip IV of Spain, Henri II of France, Henri IV of France, Emperor Ferdinand II, the Elector Palatine, and Mary Queen of Scots.

The Medici family crest—object of much historical speculation

The family symbol You come across the Medici emblem time and again in Florence—a cluster of red balls on a gold background. Yet its origins are a complete mystery. Legend claims the family were descended from Averardo, a Carolingian knight who, passing through the Mugello (south of Florence), had fought and killed a giant in battle. During the encounter his shield received six massive blows from the giant's mace. Charlemagne, as a reward for his bravery, allowed Averardo to represent the dents as red balls on his coat of arms. Others say the balls (*palle*) had less exalted origins: that they were pawnbrokers' coins, or medicinal pills (or cupping glasses) that recalled the family's origins as doctors (*medici*) or apothecaries. Others say they are *bezants*, Byzantine coins, inspired by the arms of the Arte del Cambio (the bankers' guild, to which the Medici belonged).

❏ Whatever the origin of the Medici family emblem, it is interesting to note that the number of *palle* (balls) depicted in it varied. Originally there were 12; in Cosimo de' Medici's time it was seven; the ceiling of San Lorenzo's Sagrestia Vecchia has eight; Cosimo I's tomb in the Cappelle Medicee has five; and Ferdinand's coat of arms in the Forte di Belvedere six. ❏

Cosimo de' Medici (1389–1464)
From humble origins (two wool workshops), Giovanni di Bicci had engineered a business that put the Medici in the first rank of Florentine